BEING SAFE AT HOME

BY SUSAN KESSELRING • ILLUSTRATED BY DAN McGEEHAN

The Child's World

Published by The Child's World®
1980 Lookout Drive • Mankato, MN 56003-1705
800-599-READ • www.childsworld.com

ACKNOWLEDGMENTS
The Child's World®: Mary Berendes, Publishing Director
The Design Lab: Design and production
Red Line Editorial: Editorial direction

LIBRARY OF CONGRESS CATALOGING-IN-PUBLICATION DATA
Kesselring, Susan.
 Being safe at home / by Susan Kesselring;
illustrated by Dan McGeehan.
    p. cm.
 Includes bibliographical references and index.
 ISBN 978-1-60954-299-3 (library bound: alk. paper)
 1. Home accidents—Prevention—Juvenile literature. 2. Safety
education—Juvenile literature. I. McGeehan, Dan, ill. II. Title.
 TX150.K47 2011
 613.6—dc22   2010040467

Printed in the United States of America
Mankato, MN
December, 2010
PA02069

About the Author

Susan Kesselring loves children, books, nature, and her family. She teaches K-1 students in a progressive charter school down a little country lane in Castle Rock, Minnesota. She is the mother of five daughters and lives in Apple Valley, Minnesota, with her husband, Rob, and a crazy springer spaniel named Lois Lane.

About the Illustrator

Dan McGeehan spent his younger years as an actor, author, playwright, and editor. Now he spends his days drawing, and he is much happier.

What fun things do you do at home? Are you a block builder or a car racer? Do you dress up dolls or put puzzles together? Or do you like to make popcorn or grilled cheese sandwiches with your dad?

Playing and cooking at home can be fun! You do have to be careful, though. Just remember to follow a few safety rules and you won't get hurt.

Hi! I'm Buzz B. Safe. Watch for me! I'll show you how to be safe at home.

3

Cooking is a yummy way to have fun! But be careful with hot food. Always ask an adult to take the hot food out of a microwave or an oven for you.

It is easy to cut yourself with a sharp knife. Let your mom or dad chop the vegetables and slice the bread.

Even though you can't use a knife, you can still help out at dinnertime. Offer to wash the vegetables or set the table.

6

It's great to move, skip, and dance in your home. You could trip or fall if you do not have a clear path, though. Pick up toys and keep other things off the stairs and floors. You don't want anyone else to fall, either.

Watch where you step in the bathroom or the kitchen. Water may have trickled on the floor. It could be slippery.

A rubber mat in the tub will help keep you from slipping!

Climbing trees outside is a terrific way to play. But when you're inside, climbing is not safe. Stay off tall furniture, drawers, and shelves. They could fall onto you.

Window screens keep bugs out of your home. They are not very strong, though. They will not keep you from falling out. It's safest to play away from open windows.

Always stay sitting at the table when you eat. Chew your food slowly and completely. Also, keep small objects out of your mouth. Toys, coins, balls, and balloons are not supposed to be chewed.

Keep plastic away from your head and face. Plastic covering your nose or mouth can make it hard for you to breathe.

Be careful around drapes and blinds. Their cords could twist around your neck and choke you.

A fire in the fireplace is warm and cozy. But a fire in your home is dangerous. Make a plan with your family for how to escape your home if there is a fire. Choose a spot outside where you will all meet. Practice your plan. Then you'll know what to do in a real fire.

Smoke detectors "smell" smoke before you can. Their loud alarms tell you there is a fire. You should have one on every floor of your home and near bedrooms.

Only cords should be plugged into wall **sockets**. If toys or other objects are stuck into wall sockets, you could get an electric **shock**.

Electricity moves quickly through water. If hair dryers and other things that are plugged in fall into water, they can give you an electric shock. Keep them away from sinks or tubs.

Many things used in your home are **poisons**. Cleaning products should be used only for cleaning. Ask an adult before you eat or drink anything you aren't sure about.

Some medicine looks like candy. But medicine can make you very sick if it's not yours. Even when it's your own medicine, be sure to ask an adult for help.

If a poison accidentally gets in your mouth, tell a parent right away. He or she will call a poison control center or 911 to get you help.

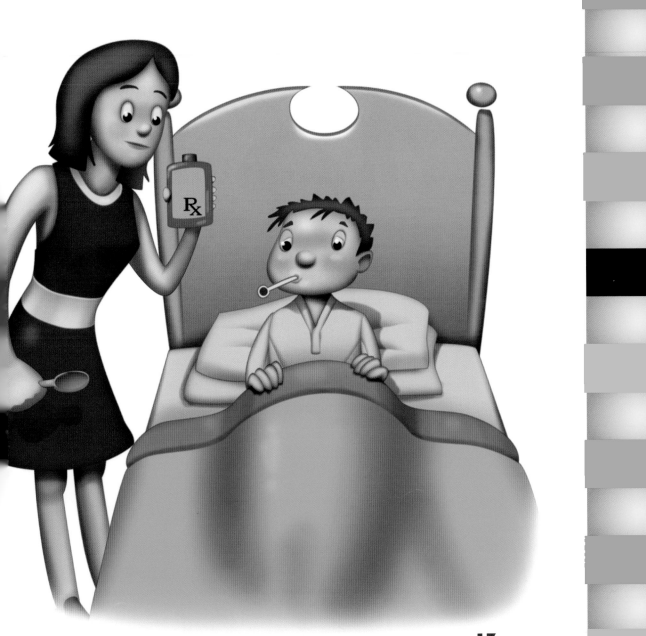

Some things at home are not for children. If you find matches or lighters, tell an adult right away. He or she can put them up high so no one gets hurt.

Do your parents have guns at home? Guns should always be locked up. If you see a gun lying around, never touch it. Run and tell an adult as fast as you can.

Do you know what to do if there is an emergency at home? Call 911. Explain the problem to the person on the phone. Sometimes he or she can tell where your call is coming from. But you may need to give the person your address. Knowing it will save precious time. He or she will send help to your house.

Learning these safety rules will keep you and your family safe at home.

If you call 911, don't hang up right away. The person may tell you instructions on what to do.

21

HOME SAFETY RULES TO REMEMBER

Always be safe!

1. Let an adult help you with hot foods and sharp knives.

2. Keep toys and other things off floors so no one trips.

3. Sit down when you are eating.

4. Keep objects that are not food out of your mouth.

5. Practice a plan for getting out of your home if there is a fire.

6. Tell an adult if you find matches, lighters, or guns.

7. Ask an adult before you eat or drink anything that is not obviously food.

8. Call 911 if there is an emergency at home.

GLOSSARY

poisons (POY-zuns): Poisons are substances that can harm or kill someone if put in the body. Some cleaning products are poisons.

shock (SHOK): A shock is the passing of electricity through someone's body. A hair dryer that touches water can cause a hurtful shock.

smoke detectors (SMOHK di-TEK-turs): Smoke detectors are devices that make loud noises to tell you there is smoke. Smoke detectors can warn you of a fire.

sockets (SOK-its): Sockets are the places in walls where you plug in electric cords. Do not put anything other than plugs in sockets.

TO LEARN MORE

BOOKS
Llewellyn, Claire. *Watch Out! At Home*. Hauppauge, New York: Barron's Educational Series, 2006.

Pancella, Peggy. *Home Safety*. Chicago: Heinemann Library, 2005.

Rau, Dana Meachen. *Safety at Home*. New York: Marshall Cavendish Benchmark, 2009.

WEB SITES
Visit our Web site for links about being safe at home:
childsworld.com/links

Note to Parents, Teachers, and Librarians: We routinely verify our Web links to make sure they are safe and active sites. So encourage your readers to check them out!